YOUR KNOWLEDGE HAS VALUE

- We will publish your bachelor's and master's thesis, essays and papers

- Your own eBook and book - sold worldwide in all relevant shops

- Earn money with each sale

Upload your text at www.GRIN.com
and publish for free

Bibliographic information published by the German National Library:

The German National Library lists this publication in the National Bibliography; detailed bibliographic data are available on the Internet at http://dnb.dnb.de .

This book is copyright material and must not be copied, reproduced, transferred, distributed, leased, licensed or publicly performed or used in any way except as specifically permitted in writing by the publishers, as allowed under the terms and conditions under which it was purchased or as strictly permitted by applicable copyright law. Any unauthorized distribution or use of this text may be a direct infringement of the author s and publisher s rights and those responsible may be liable in law accordingly.

Imprint:

Copyright © 2017 GRIN Verlag
Print and binding: Books on Demand GmbH, Norderstedt Germany
ISBN: 9783668690813

This book at GRIN:

https://www.grin.com/document/419491

Muhammad Yasir Arslan

Electoral Reforms in Pakistan. Drawing upon previous experience and building for the future

GRIN Verlag

GRIN - Your knowledge has value

Since its foundation in 1998, GRIN has specialized in publishing academic texts by students, college teachers and other academics as e-book and printed book. The website www.grin.com is an ideal platform for presenting term papers, final papers, scientific essays, dissertations and specialist books.

Visit us on the internet:

http://www.grin.com/

http://www.facebook.com/grincom

http://www.twitter.com/grin_com

ELECTORAL REFORMS IN PAKISTAN
"Drawing upon previous experience and building for the future"

Will recently proposed electoral reforms and relevant suggestions of international election observers improve the election procedures in Pakistan and enhance its public confidence on coming future elections OR will it remain unfunctional and unsuccessful similar to its all previous reforms?

BY: MUHAMMAD YASIR ARSLAN

1. **BACKGROUND AND INTRODUCTION:**

State elections are believed to be backbone of democratic countries' legislature systems which provide their citizens a legal chance to select their representatives through fair and free procedures within their constitutional and administrative frame works. These organizational frameworks are required to be autonomous, unbiased, efficient, effective by regular reviews and necessary modifications under modern administrative and managerial measures. This is not only to ensure compliance with international standards and obligations but also to reflect a wider political system, to involve public participation and to maintain their confidence in the efficiency of the improved democratic system. It has been further observed that political and democratic structures are always strengthened by ensuring receptive and comprehensive electoral processes. Additionally, fair and free election process generally increases electorates' confidence on electoral system. Also, candidates easily accept the results without major blames on the opponents and allegations on election commissioners.

Almost after 70 years of its independence from United Kingdom in 1947, Pakistani government yet failed to conduct a single fair election through unanimously accepted voting process by its public. In fact, final results of elections were challenged many time by losing parties based on their complaints of election rigging due to bogus old fashioned voting system. This situation was found more worsen during the last election held in 2013, when all political parties blamed for ballot theft and party voters were on streets for their political protests. The rigging allegations have been a common phenomenon in Pakistan over the period. Consequently, despite of the political and social differences; there is recognition among all local and international stakeholders that electoral reforms are vital and essential to sustain democracy in Pakistan. Poorer and bogus electoral process gives birth to a weaker government which invites non-democratic elements like Military and religious groups to take over to control government. This practice is more common in

Pakistani political and social culture therefore, its constitution was breached by Martial laws several times.

2. DEFINITION AND ARGUMENTS OF ELECTORAL REFORMS:

Many types of reforms exist and hence their definitions can mean many things. Different experts and authors have defined reforms differently based on their academic research and understanding on social, fiscal, administrational, managerial, organisational, political and economic set-ups. Pollitt and Bouckaert in 2011 defined reform as 'deliberate changes to the structures and processes of public sector organizations with the objective of getting them (in some sense) to run better'. In 2002, Michael Barzelay explained that 'macro-level reform is about re-designing systems, or 'public management policy' to transform institutions and the rules of the game (reformist model)' while it was Janine O'Flynn in 2015 who argued that 'currently, our thinking on reform focuses on distinct levels of analysis but not on the whole picture. Moving forward, we must begin to think about reform differently as a much more interrelated and dynamic series of processes' [1]. Doug McTaggart further added in 2015 that 'reform is never far from the centre of public administration practice. Also, true and lasting reform is not easy, given the resilience of the status quo' [2]. As per Steven Van & Gerhard (2011), 'many reforms are not clear-cut but rather emerge or remain undefined and combine many New Public Management (NPM) and non-NPM-style reform elements' [3].

Political setup and its developing history differs from country to country. For few country social, political and administrative reforms are slower and lesser effective than others due to its governmental structure, financial condition and literacy rates. This is common in sub-continental countries like Pakistan, Srilanka, Bangladesh, Bhutan and Maldives.

3. ELECTORAL ARRANGEMENT IN PAKISTAN:

Pakistan is a federation with 4 federating units (provinces) who operate under a common Law judicial system like UK, Australia and Canada. Further, separation of power is also similar of UK,

Australia i.e. legislatures, executive and judiciary. Under Pakistani constitutional frame of work, elections are to be held after each 5 year which in fact more often happened earlier before completing the tenure of government. Majority election system (non-presidential and non-proportional representation system) is method of state election and provincial elections in Pakistan. President as head of state, elected by national assembly/ federal parliaments while prime minter acts as head of government who always elected by federal parliament. Chief ministers elected by provincial assemblies of each province. Unlike Australia, Pakistani election is based on first-past-the-post voting method instead of preferential voting.

4. **HISTORY OF ELECTIONS IN PAKISTAN:**

In Pakistan, up till now total 11 Elections held from 1962 to 2013. For first 15 years after its independence in 1947 from British Monarch, no elections were held in Pakistan. After its first ever election of 1962, 10 more elections were held in randomly in 1965, 1970, 1977, 1985, 1988, 1990, 1993, 1997, 2002, 2008 and 2013. The federal elections of 1970 are generally considered the fairest elections in the history of Pakistan and unfortunately, all remaining elections were failed and fixed.

5. **OBSERVATIONS OF NATIONAL AND INTERNATIONAL ELECTION OBSERVERS:**

United nation and other international and national organisations have been observing the Pakistani electoral procedures, shadowy areas requiring necessary election improvement (long term and short term) and the fairness of overall electoral system to strengthen democracy and government structures. In a nationwide survey by **UN Development Programme (UNDP)**, it was concluded that about 49% voters were not satisfied with the existing electoral system while 55% electorates requested local government for electoral reforms.

European Union Election Observer Mission (EUEOMs) notified their observations as "fundamental problems remain with the legal framework and the implementation of certain provisions, leaving future processes vulnerable to malpractice and Pakistan not fully meeting its obligations to provide citizens the right and opportunity to stand as candidates and to vote." [4]

As per findings of **Free and Fair Election Network (FAFEN)**, the voter turnout was more than 100% in at least 49 polling stations out of sampled 8,120 polling stations across Pakistan which clearly indicate bogus voting and failure of election process. **Pakistan Institute of Legislative Development and Transparency (PILDAT) also pointed out that** 'though charges of small scale rigging and irregularities were levelled by different political parties and individuals, the overall quality of elections showed a considerable improvement'. [5]

Public Interests in Election: Notwithstanding, voters showed a great interest in recent 2013 election expecting for a complete change in Pakistani political and electoral system but it was unsuccessful due to uninterrupted corrupt practices and lack of accountability and absence of transparency. Failure of fair and free election again caused huge disappointment amongst voters and effected the public participation in the following by-elections. Almost all the major political parties complained and protested for extra ballot papers' printing, election rigging, missing papers and bogus votes which further aggravated the political condition in Pakistan. An extremely low voter turn-out was observed due to lack of trust in the following by-elections. This weak credibility of the electoral system is the heart of the weak political system and mother of all evil practices in Pakistan.

6. **KEY ISSUES TO UNSUCCESSFUL ELECTIONS AND SYSTEM FAILURE:**

The Election Commission of Pakistan (ECP) was formed in 1956 who by its function must be an independent and autonomous federal institute, responsible for organizing and conducting state parliament, provincial legislatures and local governments elections. ECP has a 5-member panel (retired Judges), out of which 4 members are from each of the four provinces (equal representation irrespective of population to avoid any administrative and constitutional conflict).

Bureaucracy, executive and legislatures all are equal responsible for the system failure in Pakistan and this is the main reason that why ECP has remained outdated and incurable so far.

Further, appointment of the chief election commissioner and the four ECP members by political parties is also a major fact of fixed election. It is always remained un-natural for people in power to make enhancements and reformative actions that will abolish their own political and financial prospects through election fairness and public participation. Current setup of ECP is partially controlled by executives and it is evidently dysfunctional by the establishment. Nepotism and favoritism have been destroying its organizational function over the time. Overall, it is an institutional failure which does not have any will for its positive reform and therefore, entire electoral procedures need to be redesigned.

7. **COUNTRY ELECTORAL REFORMS AND MAJOR SUGGESTIONS:**

Taking into consideration of observers' suggestions, previous lessons learned and social needs, electoral reforms were drafted. Many are concerned to public sector reform in which ECP institutional improvement and its financial and managerial autonomy are included while other large portion of reforms are reflected election process fairness and evaluation processes through new public value model in which people participation is considered necessary during decision-making of an institutional reforms and its restructuring. The Election Commission of Pakistan (ECP) prepared and unveiled a 5-year strategic 2010-2014 to improve the election process as part of electoral reforms meeting international election standards consists of total of 129 objectives are listed under 15 strategic goals [6].

THE ELECTION COMMISSION OF PAKISTAN (ECP) PROPOSED ELECTORAL REFORMS

Sr. No.	Strategic Goals	No. of Objective	Objectives' outputs
1	Improving legal framework for elections	4	Legal framework committee was formed
2	Improving the election operations	19	Simplification of election-related forms and utilizing of Electronic Voting Machines (EVMs)
3	Improvement in the registration of voters and preparation of credible, accurate, up-to-date and accessible electoral rolls	12	Computerized electoral rolls
4	Establishing an effective and transparent election complaints and disputes resolution mechanism	4	Designation of officers to deal with complaints
5	Restructuring the election commission of Pakistan	7	Re-organization plan of ECP at the secretariat, provincial, divisional and districts levels (partial decentralization)
6	Improving the infrastructure, logistics and equipment for ECP offices	11	Government and international donors for funding.
7	Improving the human resources of ECP	10	A detailed human resource policy was developed
8	Attaining complete financial autonomy and appropriate funding for ECP	4	Similar to legislatures
9	Institutionalizing training, research evaluation in ECP	18	18 Training manuals and handbooks were developed, more positions were created for strengthening the federal election academy
10	Promoting the use of IT in ECP operation	8	Objectives, a comprehensive IT policy for ECP was formulated in line with NADRA including re-design of website.
11	Improving the public outreach and interaction with political parties, civil society and the media	5	ECP established two Political consultative forum and civil, society consultative forum and consulted them in EVMs and reforms. Permanent media centre
12	Strengthening of participation of political parties and candidates	6	Appropriate legal amendments to improve transparency of political finance. Committed to upload annual statement of assets and liabilities by all legislatures on the ECP website
13	Enhancing the participation of voters and improving the civic and voters education	10	Enhance the voters turnout from 44% up to 63% by civic and voters education strategies.
14	Improving the participation of marginalised groups including women, minorities and persons with disabilities in the electoral process	6	To support the adoption of legislation on participation of persons particularly transgender.
15	Creating a refreshing and dynamic branding of the election commission	3	A distinct and uniform design for the divisional and districts buildings and signboards.

Author's own works: table developed based on the information available at:
Source: Election Commission of Pakistan, Five-Year Strategic Plan 2010-2014, issued on 25 May 2010, <https://www.ecp.gov.pk/>
PILDAT report, 2011, Sate of Electoral Reforms in Pakistan, p.7,
<http://www.pildat.org/publications/publication/elections/StateOfElectoralReformsInPakistan_CitizensMonitoringReport.pdf/>

Main suggestions towards electoral reforms revolve around institutional, financial, managerial, technological and societal reforms, through which people of all sects can participate in elections and vote their candidates, knowing their issues and representing their rights. These are based on the following initiatives:

- A new national census to verify voters and to reconstitute the fresh boundaries of electoral constituencies ensuring equal representation irrespective of land area.
- Election commission members must be selected through parliamentary voting.
- Needs to replace the old voting system with proportional representation to ensure true representation in proportion to legislatures' strength in their electorates.
- No more elections without Electronic Voting Machines (EVMs).
- Parliament's term to be reduced to 3 years which would provide more chances of accountability of politicians by voters in case of their representatives' poor performance.
- Check and control on the candidate expenses during the election campaign to give equal chances to more people with lesser budgets.
- To guarantee electoral reforms are accurately implemented, full independence and sufficient resources to Election Commission (EC) by strengthening its autonomous authority.

8. REFERENCES:

1. O' Flynn Janine, 2015, *Public Sector Reform: The Puzzle We Can Never Solve?*. Available at: http://content.ebscohost.com.ezproxy.canberra.edu.au/ContentServer.asp
2. McTaggart Doug, 2015. *Public Sector Reform: Business as Usual is Not an Option* Available at: http://content.ebscohost.com.ezproxy.canberra.edu.au/ContentServer.asp
3. Steven Van de Walle and Gerhard Hammerschmid. 2011. "The Impact of the New Public Management: Challenges for Coordination and Cohesion in European Public Sectors." *Halduskultuur – Administrative Culture* 12 (2), 190-209
4. UNDP, 2014, *Electoral Reforms in Pakistan: Perspectives and Opportunities*. Available at: http://reliefweb.int/report/pakistan/electoral-reforms-pakistan-perspectives-and-opportunities
5. PILDAT report, 2011, *Sate of Electoral Reforms in Pakistan*. Available at: http://www.pildat.org/publications/publication/elections/StateOfElectoralReformsInPakistan_CitizensMonitoringReport.pdf/
6. The News, 2015, *How to improve electoral system in Pakistan*. Available at: https://forpakistan.org/how-to-improve-electoral-system-in-pakistan/

YOUR KNOWLEDGE HAS VALUE

- We will publish your bachelor's and master's thesis, essays and papers

- Your own eBook and book - sold worldwide in all relevant shops

- Earn money with each sale

Upload your text at www.GRIN.com
and publish for free